S0-BKC-539

OLYSLAGER AUTO LIBRARY

Buses and Coaches
from 1940

compiled by the OLYSLAGER ORGANISATION
edited by Bart H. Vanderveen

FREDERICK WARNE & Co Ltd
London and New York

THE OLYSLAGER AUTO LIBRARY

This book is one of a growing range of titles on major transport subjects. Titles published so far include:

The Jeep
Half-Tracks
Scammell Vehicles
Fire-Fighting Vehicles
Earth-Moving Vehicles
Wreckers and Recovery Vehicles
Passenger Vehicles 1893–1940
Buses and Coaches from 1940
Fairground and Circus Transport

American Cars of the 1930s
American Cars of the 1940s
American Cars of the 1950s

British Cars of the Early Thirties
British Cars of the Late Thirties
British Cars of the Early Forties
British Cars of the Late Forties

Library of Congress Catalog Card No. 73-89825

ISBN 0 7232 1754 8

Filmset and printed in Great Britain
by BAS Printers Limited, Wallop, Hampshire

575. 873

INTRODUCTION

This volume supplements our book 'Passenger Vehicles 1893–1940', and provides a survey of buses and coaches that were produced from 1940 until the present day. It covers, by random selection, the products of a large number of manufacturers from all over the world. Many of the vehicles consist of chassis produced by one manufacturer and bodywork by another, but it will be seen that increasing numbers of buses and coaches are supplied as complete units by single suppliers or groups of suppliers. The former include firms where the complete vehicle is made, e.g. Daimler-Benz, or where the engine and other mechanical components are acquired by the builder from an outside source, e.g. Van Hool in Belgium, who use Fiat automotive components for many of their models. The latter are corporations where one division builds the automotive parts and another the bodywork, a good example being a Park Royal-bodied AEC, both companies being members of the British Leyland Corporation.

Most modern public transport vehicles have forward control, rear-mounted diesel engine, driving the rear axle through an automatic or semi-automatic transmission system, pneumatic (air) suspension and dual-circuit air brakes. In spite of this sophisticated specification it cannot always be said that the quality is as it used to be. Purchase price now being a primary consideration in virtually every transport fleet, manufacturers, in order to be competitive, cannot afford apparently to take as much care over finish and materials as in earlier days. A comparison of detail between a modern London double-decker bus and old stalwarts such as the 'RT'-type and the 'Routemaster' (many of which are still in service) will prove this point.

However, the fierce competition between the world's leading suppliers and the stringent requirements from the operators have produced a range of most interesting designs, particularly in the field of long-distance and city buses, and ultra-luxurious touring coaches.

Piet Olyslager MSIA, MSAE, KIVI

AEC

4A AEC/Verheul 'Polyrama'

4B AEC/Harrington 'Granadier'

4A: **AEC/Verheul** 'Polyrama' coach of the 1964 series of the NV Auto-Industrie Verheul of Gouda, Netherlands (later the Dutch subsidiary of British Leyland). Based on the 'Reliance' chassis, it was available with either the AH470 135-bhp or the AH590 150-bhp engine, both horizontal six-cylinder diesels. There were interior layouts for 36 to 53 passengers.
4B: **AEC** 'Reliance' chassis, Model 2U3RA with manual gearbox, air brakes and AH590 engine. The 49/51-seater bodywork was by Harrington and was one of the last produced by this firm. 1965.
4C: **AEC/Plaxton** 'Panorama Elite' of 1969, a modern coach with luxury accommodation for 57 passengers on an AEC 12-metre chassis. The complete vehicle cost £8750, the bare chassis £3500.

4C AEC/Plaxton 'Panorama Elite'

5A: **AEC** 'Merlin' chassis was based on the rear-engined 'Swift' design and was available with AH505 or AH691 diesel engine, four-speed semi- or fully-automatic transmission and 16 ft 6 in or 18 ft 6 in wheelbase. This is a London Transport 'Red Arrow' one-man-operated bus of 1966.
5B: **AEC** 'Swift' o-m-o bus in Nottingham, 1969. This bus was powered by the 151-bhp Model AH505 engine, driving through a semi-automatic transmission.
5C: **AEC** 'Swift' with single-deck bodywork by Park Royal, operated by London Transport, 1970. Like AEC, Park Royal, old-established coachbuilders, are part of the British Leyland Motor Corporation. This picture was taken at Chiswick.

5A AEC 'Merlin'

5B AEC 'Swift'

5C AEC 'Swift'

AEC

6A AEC 'Routemaster'

6B AEC 'Regent'

6C AEC 'Renown'

6A: No doubt one of the world's best known buses: the London Transport **AEC** 'Routemaster'. The engine was an AEC 128-bhp 9·6-litre diesel, driving through a fluid flywheel and electro-pneumatically-operated direct-acting four-speed epicyclic gearbox. The bodywork, by Park Royal Vehicles Ltd, was of aluminium alloy integral construction employing the stressed skin principle throughout. The mechanical units (engine, axles, etc.) were attached directly to the body structure. The bonnet was a fibre-glass reinforced plastic moulding. Seating capacity: upper saloon 36, lower saloon 28. Dimensions: length 27 ft 6 in, width 8 ft, wheelbase 16 ft 10 in. Unladen weight just over seven tons. 1958–64.

6B: **AEC** 'Regent' Mk V of 1960, with double-deck bodywork by Park Royal Vehicles Ltd for East Kent. The 'Regent' Mk V chassis was in production in several variants (Models LD2LA, D2RA, D3RV, etc.) from 1955 until December 1964, during which period 2835 units were delivered.

6C: **AEC** 'Renown' with 74-seater Park Royal bodywork. This low-height model, which featured one-step front entrance, rear air suspension and offset transmission line, appeared at the Earl's Court Commercial Motor Show in London in 1962.

ALBION, AM GENERAL, AUSTIN

7A Albion 'Venturer'

7C AM General/Flyer

7B Albion 'Viking'

7D Austin

7A: **Albion** 'Venturer' Model CX19 of 1948. This Cheltenham & District-operated rear-entrance double-decker had 56-seat bodywork by Metro-Cammell.

7B: **Albion** rear-engined 'Viking' of 1967, operated by Walter Alexander & Co (Midland) Ltd. The 40-seater semi-coach bodywork was by W. Alexander & Co (Coachbuilders) Ltd of Falkirk, Stirlingshire, Scotland..

7C: In 1971 **AM General Corp.,** a wholly owned subsidiary of American Motors Corp., and Flyer Industries of Winnipeg, Canada, reached agreement granting AM General worldwide rights to build and market Flyer diesel and electric city transit buses and diesel-powered intercity buses. Flyer Industries Ltd (formerly Western Flyer Coach, Ltd) are America's largest producers of electric transit buses, an example of which is shown.

7D: **Austin** 14-seater passenger-cum-mail bus of 1946, operated until the 1960s by Angus MacPhee on the Isle of Skye. It was based on a petrol-engined SWB chassis.

BARREIROS, BEADLE

8A: The Spanish firm of **Barreiros**, founded in 1954, was re-organized in 1970 as Chrysler Espana SA, a subsidiary of the Chrysler Corporation. This 1970 'Autobus Interurbano 6.000' had accommodation for 59+2 persons and a wheelbase of 6 metres. The Barreiros BH-26 diesel engine developed 170 bhp at 2200 rpm, and either a Wilson or a ZF gearbox could be fitted.
8B: **Beadle/Leyland** 35-seater coach of 1952. This was a semi-chassisless vehicle, using pre-war Leyland 'Titan' TD5 running components. Messrs John C. Beadle (Coachbuilders) Ltd of Dartford, Kent, produced a variety of (semi-) chassisless buses and coaches, later incorporating Rootes running gear. During 1955–57 these were marketed under the Beadle marque name (see 8C).
8C: One of a batch of 12 **Beadle** 36-seater continental touring coaches supplied in 1955/56 to Smith's Tours (Wigan) Ltd. A Rootes TS3 two-stroke diesel powered the vehicle, and the bodywork was designed and produced by Beadle.

8B Beadle/Leyland

8A Barreiros 6.000

8C Beadle Mk O.E.II

9A: During the war years Vauxhall Motors produced some 3398 **Bedford** OWB bus chassis for essential civilian use. Mechanically they were similar to the peace-time Model OB (174-inch wheelbase, 3·5-litre six-cylinder OHV petrol engine, servo-assisted brakes, etc.) but the 32-seat bodywork was of the Utility type, very austere and devoid of any bright work.
9B: **Bedford** truck chassis are often used for low-cost buses, particularly overseas. This is a 28-seater on the 151-inch wheelbase Model KE (Series TK) chassis, by Marshall of Cambridge. It was supplied in 1970 to Broomfield Hospital, Chelmsford, for staff transportation.
9C: **Bedford** Series CA was in production from 1952 until 1969 when it was replaced by the CF. There were personnel-carrying variants of both. This is a 1963 CALV (LWB) Martin Walter 'Utilabrake', used as a mini-bus by W. Sutherland, Isle of Skye.
9D: **Bedford/Duple** 'Vista 25' coach, based on the 164-inch wheelbase Model VAS chassis, supplied in 1970 to the National Cash Register Co.

9A Bedford OWB

9C Bedford CALV

9B Bedford KE

9D Bedford/Duple 'Vista 25'

BEDFORD

10A: **Bedford** SB passenger chassis with 1959 'Super Vega' 37-passenger coach bodywork by Duple Motor Bodies Ltd of The Hyde, Hendon, London, NW9.
10B: **Bedford** VAS was a short-wheelbase bus and coach chassis, available with 300 or 330 CID diesel (VAS-1) or 214 CID petrol engine (VAS-2). Shown is a 1962 Duple 29-seater luxury coach, designed specifically to meet PSV operators' needs for a medium-sized vehicle, combining economy with manoeuvrability. The two-ton body was of composite construction and had a 60-cu. ft rear luggage locker.
10C: **Bedford** VAM was a medium-wheelbase passenger chassis, used by many coachbuilders. The example shown was produced by Duple for Starduster Coaches in 1966 and is seen taking part in the 12th British Coach Rally to Brighton.
10D: **Bedford** Model YRT 12-metre 53-seat chassis appeared in 1972. This example has Willowbrook 002 'Express Bus' coachwork. Key design feature of the YRT was the Bedford approach to 'amidships' engine location, first introduced in the 45-seat Model YRQ chassis of 1970 (which was developed from the VAM). The YRT has a Bedford 446 CID diesel, 222-inch WB, PAS and full-air brakes with separate circuits serving front and rear wheels.

10A Bedford/Duple 'Super Vega'

10C Bedford/Duple 'Bella Venture'

10B Bedford/Duple 'Bella Vista'

10D Bedford/Willowbrook 002

11A: The **Bedford** Model VAL twin-steer Leyland-engined 52/55-seater passenger chassis made its public debut on 14 September 1962. The manufacturers, Vauxhall Motors, said that safety, comfort and economy had been the primary aims in its design. It was intended to accommodate 36-ft long luxury coach and service bus bodies, but has also been used for special bodywork such as large furniture vans, horse transporters, etc.

11B: **Bedford** VAL-based Plaxton 'Panorama' 52-seater coach of 1965 on full lock in the 12th British Coach Rally. The coach was entered by Kenzie's Coaches Ltd of Shepreth, Cambs and driven by Mr C. B. Kenzie, winner of the Coach Driver of the Year Award.

11C: **Bedford** VAL air passenger buses supplied in 1966 to Trans World Airways for airport use. Note the large central entry/exit doors, the lengthwise seats and the roof observation windows.

11A Bedford VAL

11B Bedford/Plaxton 'Panorama'

11C Bedford VAL

BERLIET, BORGWARD, BRISTOL

12A: Automobiles M. **Berliet** are among the leading manufacturers of passenger vehicles and heavy-duty trucks in France. Illustrated is a 'Cruisair 2' coach, 'Grand Tourisme' model, with 32 seats and 200-bhp diesel engine. At the other end of the scale Berliet offer articulated city buses for up to 200 passengers.
12B: **Borgward** B2000 diesel truck chassis with soft-top personnel carrier bodywork were in service with German police forces during the Fifties. A slightly smaller (12-seater) model was based on Hanomag L28 chassis.
12C: **Bristol** 55-seater Lowbridge Double-Deck bus of Thames Valley, 1946. Bodywork was by Eastern Coach Works Ltd of Lowestoft.
12D: **Bristol** RELL 6G Gardner diesel-engined chassis with 50-seater RELL Stage Carriage Single-Deck body produced in aluminium alloy by ECW, in 1966, for United Automobile Services Ltd of Darlington, Co. Durham. Bristol chassis at this time were supplied only for nationalized operating companies.

12A Berliet 'Cruisair 2'

12B Borgward B2000

12C Bristol K

12D Bristol RELL6G

13A: **Bristol** 70-passenger bus with aluminium alloy body by ECW, supplied to the City of Oxford Motor Services Ltd in 1970. The rear-mounted Gardner 6LX 135-bhp diesel drove through a semi-automatic five-speed gearbox. Wheelbase was 194 inches, tyre size 10.00-20. Control of ECW (Eastern Coach Works) was passed to the National Bus Company in 1969, and in 1970 they formed, together with British Leyland, Bus Manufacturers (Holdings) of which ECW formed part, and in which both NBC and BLMC retained a 50% interest. Today these companies, as well as Bristol, are members of British Leyland's Truck and Bus Division.
13B: **Büssing** re-started immediately after the destruction of the 1939–45 war with the production of their Model 5000S normal-control truck and 5000T forward-control bus. Early models were very austere, but by 1951 the 5000T bus looked like this. The engine was a Model LD 105-bhp six-cylinder diesel of 7413 cc, with five-speed overdrive gearbox.
13C: **Büssing** Trambus, designated 'Senator', had underfloor diesel engine at rear and was available during the Sixties with several seating configurations and variations in wheelbase, transmission, etc. The '13D' version, for up to 113 passengers, is shown here.

13B Büssing 5000T

13A Bristol VRT/SL

13C Büssing 'Senator'

BÜSSING

14A Büssing 'Senator'

14C Büssing/Emmelmann 'Präsident'

14B Büssing/Emmelmann 'Präsident'

14A: **Büssing** 'Senator' 12 operating in Essen. This city bus could be supplied with capacity of either 95 persons (37 seating, 58 standing) or 102 persons (44 and 58 resp.). The overall length was 10·76 metres, the wheelbase 5·40. Engine was 7·4 litre 150-bhp six-cylinder diesel.
14B: **Büssing** offered a range of articulated buses for city and country use. They were produced in conjunction with Emmelmann in Hannover, who built the bodywork. The engine was horizontally mounted within the wheelbase of the leading unit. The city bus shown was operated by the Essener Verkehrs-AG.
14C: **Büssing/Emmelmann** 'Präsident' BS170N was one of four models available in 1970. The BS170N was intended for country use (*Überlandlinienverkehr*) and was 16·9 metres long. It could accommodate 157 passengers, i.e. 71 seating and 86 standing. The engine was the Büssing U11D of 185 or 210 bhp. Several transmission systems could be specified, including Voith-Diwabus automatic.

15A Chevrolet Series BG

15B Chevrolet Series TL

15C Chevrolet

15A: In 1942 a number of five-passenger cars were converted in the USA to military 15-seater buses. Here is one of 100 **Chevrolet** sedans being converted by S.L. Savidge, Dodge-Plymouth dealer in Seattle, Wash. Masonite, wood and other 'non-strategic' materials were used for the insert frame and two additional doors on the right. (See also *The Observer's Fighting Vehicles Directory—World War II*.)
15B: **Chevrolet** TL4502 'Loadmaster' 161-in wheelbase chassis with bus bodywork produced by Rowlands Ltd in Colombo, Ceylon, in 1950. The body was built with native labour, utilizing Bonallack light-alloy framing imported from Britain. The OHV Six petrol engine drove through a four-speed gearbox.
15C: **Chevrolet** 1973 bus chassis comprise the familiar truck-type school bus chassis for capacities of up to 66 students (bodywork by Wayne, Superior, Carpenter, Ward, Thomas, Blue Bird, etc.), and three rear-engined forward-control special chassis. The former are available with Six, V6 or V8 petrol engine or V6 diesel, the latter with four sizes of V6 petrol engines.

CITROËN, COMMER

16A Citroën/Heuliez

16C Commer FC

16B Commer Q4 'Commando'

16D Commer/BTC

16A: **Citroën** of France offered bus chassis of several types, including the 5·33-metre wheelbase T55, shown here with 1965 lightweight body by Louis Heuliez of Cerizay. Petrol and diesel six-cylinder engines were available, with five- or four-speed gearbox.
16B: The **Commer** 'Commando' 20-seater 'deck-and-a-half' coach was used mainly for transport of air passengers. Under the upper deck, or observation saloon, was a large luggage compartment. Engine was 90-bhp L-head Six, gearbox four-speed, WB 15 ft 9 in. Body by Park Royal, 1947.

16C: **Commer** FC 7-ton truck chassis/scuttle with locally-produced bodywork, operating in the north of Thailand, from Chiang Mai, 1956.
16D: This semi-trailer bus was operated by the Bahrein Petroleum Company Ltd. The tractor was a mid-Fifties 12-ton **Commer** FC Mk III unit with underfloor engine, and the 100-seater semi-trailer was built by the British Trailer Company. The semi-trailer type should not be confused with the articulated configuration where the actual bus body is of the centrally-'hinged' walk-through type.

17A Commer 'Superpoise'

17D Commer 'Superpoise'

17B Commer 'Superpoise'

17C Commer 'Superpoise'

17E Commer 'Walk-Thru'

17A: **Commer** 'Superpoise' of 1948, operated by Mkikimbe Bus Service of Maidstone, Natal. Chassis was 13 ft 11 in WB Model QD465 4/5-tonner with Perkins P6 diesel. Body was locally-produced all-metal 34-seater.
17B **Commer** 'Superpoise' 4-ton chassis with 24-seater coachwork, produced in the Netherlands in the early Fifties. Note the modified outer sections of the front wings.
17C: **Commer** 'Superpoise' Mk IV, operated by Motor Transport Ltd of Georgetown, British Guiana. Body was built by local labour at the Tractor & Motor Company's Service Dept in Georgetown, 1959.
17D: **Commer** 'Superpoise' $1\frac{1}{2}$-ton Model BD3024 chassis with 17-seater bodies operated by the Sarawak Transport Company in Kuching, North Borneo. Powered by 2·26-litre 4-cyl. Rootes diesels, the chassis were supplied by Lyons Motors of Singapore, *c.* 1960.
17E: **Commer** 'Walk-Thru' chassis with 22-seater school bus bodywork by Nielson of Asnaes and operated in the Faeroe Isles in the Sixties.

COMMER

18A: **Commer** 'Avenger' was bus chassis version of the well-known FC truck chassis with underfloor engine (petrol or diesel). It is shown here with Danish bodywork of the early Fifties.

18B: **Commer** 'Avenger' with typical Belgian bodywork (by Carrosserie Jonckheere) of the early Fifties, featuring the ubiquitous 'portholes' of the period.

18C: **Commer** 'Avenger', one of five Beadle-bodied 39-seaters in service with The Jalan Langgar Transport Co of Alor Star, the capital of Kedah on the West Coast of the Malay Peninsula. 1954.

18D: **Commer** 'Avenger' combined 14-passenger and 2-ton load carrying vehicle supplied in Norway, in 1955. Bodywork was produced locally and vehicle was powered by the Rootes TS3 two-stroke diesel.

18E: **Commer** 'Avenger' 37-seater coach with Danish bodywork, supplied to coach operators Selandia through the Danish Rootes Group distributors British Motors AS in the Fifties.

18F: **Commer** 'Avenger'-based 'Fiesta' 41-passenger coach by W. S. Yeates Ltd of Loughborough, Leics. It was supplied to Moss Motor Tours, Isle of Wight, in May, 1961.

18B Commer 'Avenger'

18D Commer 'Avenger'

18C Commer 'Avenger'

18E Commer 'Avenger'

18A Commer 'Avenger'

18F Commer 'Avenger'

COMMER/BEADLE, CROSSLEY, DAF

19A Commer/Beadle

19C DAF B1300

19A: **Beadle** produced this 35-seater chassisless coach in 1953 to their own design, using **Commer** mechanical components, including the TS3 diesel engine. It was hired to several operators, among them Maidstone and District Motor Services, in whose livery it is seen here. (See also page 8.)

19B: **Crossley** DD42/5, supplied to Eastbourne Corporation in 1949. The 56-seat rear-entrance bodywork was by East Lancs. Engine was a Crossley six-cylinder diesel.

19C: **DAF**, the Dutch motor vehicle manufacturers, started truck production in 1948 and soon introduced bus and coach chassis derivations. This is a late-Fifties Model B1300 chassis for 32- to 36-seaters, available with 120-bhp diesel or 135-bhp petrol engine. Coachwork shown was by NV Carrosserie Roset of Bergen op Zoom for the operators van Asten's Tours.

19D: One of the latest passenger chassis offered by **DAF** is the DKDL variant of the underfloor-engined MB200. The horizontal 11·6-litre six-cylinder diesel develops 165 DIN-bhp. The bodywork was designed specifically for inter-urban or city bus service. The specimen shown is in service with the LTM in Limburg, the most southern province of the Netherlands.

19B Crossley DD42/5

19D DAF MB200DKDL

DAIMLER

20A : **Daimler** 50-seat half-deck coach, supplied to Don Everall Ltd, Wolverhampton, in 1953. The rather unusual bodywork was by Mann Egerton & Co Ltd of Norwich.
20B : **Daimler** 77-seat rear-engined 'Fleetline' was the first new vehicle announced after the firm's take-over by Jaguar in 1960. The staircase was behind the driver. WB 16 ft 3 in.

20C : **Daimler** introduced their Cummins-engined 'Roadliner' in 1964. Shown is one of 31 supplied in 1966 to Transit Systems of Edmonton and Calgary, Alberta, Canada.
20D : **Daimler** Fleetline o-m-o double-decker for Manchester City Transport, 1968. These had 16 ft 9 in WB. Gardner 6LX 150-bhp diesel drove through 'Daimatic' epicyclic gearbox.

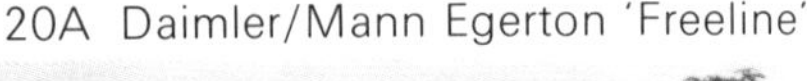
20A Daimler/Mann Egerton 'Freeline'

20B Daimler/MCW 'Fleetline'

20C Daimler/Willowbrook 'Roadliner'

20D Daimler/Park Royal 'Fleetline'

21A: **Dennis** 'Lancet' J3 chassis with 47–51-seat coachwork by Park Royal, delivered in 1950 to East Kent. This chassis, powered by a Dennis 'oiler', was sold in large quantities for bus and coach applications.
21B: **Dennis** 'Loline' YF6 double-decker chassis with 70-seat bodywork by Northern Counties, one of a batch delivered in 1960 to Middlesborough Corporation Transport (now part of the Teesside Transport Authority). Engine was a Gardner 6LW.
21C: **Dodge** Brothers (Britain) Ltd of Kew, Surrey, introduced a new forward entry 42-seater service bus in 1962. It had a Leyland 0·370 diesel engine and metal construction bodywork by MCW, incorporating Dodge Kew truck type radiator grille. Chassis cost £1920.
21D: **Dodge** 29-seater of the typical American 'school bus' style in service with the US Air Force in the UK (RHD, 1964). It was one of several types available. The front end styling was of the 1962 pattern and continued for several years (it was used also by Dodge in Great Britain, 1963–67).

21A Dennis/Park Royal 'Lancet'

21C Dodge/MCW

21B Dennis/Northern Counties 'Loline'

21D Dodge S8-S500/Blue Bird

FIAT, FLXIBLE

22A: The six-wheeled Italian **Fiat** 672RN 'Autobus' was in production during 1948–52 and was a 12-metre city bus for 100 passengers. It had rear entrance and forward exit. The engine was a 123-bhp 10·17-litre six-cylinder Fiat 368 diesel, driving through a dual range four-speed transmission (4F1R×2).

22B: **Fiat** 60-passenger 404UP 'Autobus' as produced during 1954–58. The engine was a 6650-cc six-cylinder diesel which drove through a four-speed gearbox, giving a maximum speed of about 53 km/h. Full air brakes acted on the four wheels, all of which were shod with 5–22 Michelin 'Metalics'. WB was 4·40 metres, length 8·50 metres.

22C: **Fiat** Model 314 based urban bus, produced by Pistoiesi Officine Meccaniche Ferroviarie SpA of Pistoia, Italy. Note the square styling, providing maximum capacity within compact overall dimensions. 1970/71.

22D: The **Flxible** Company of Loudonville, Ohio, is one of the biggest volume-producers of integral rear-engined buses and coaches in the USA. This is a typical long-distance coach of about 1960. Note the tinted glass and the riveted construction of the outer skin, following aircraft practice.

22A Fiat 672 RN

22B Fiat 404UP

22C Fiat/Pistoiesi

22D Flxible

23A: **Flxible** 'Flxiliner' DeLuxe Intercity coach, Model 223DD-D2, of 1971. It is powered by a 238-bhp Detroit Diesel engine, mounted at the rear, and features independent front suspension, Flxilastic torque rubber springs and aluminium wheels. Capacity is 41–45 passengers.
23B: **Flxible** 40-ft transit coach with front entrance (note 'Welcome Aboard' sign) and centre exit. Two-cycle Detroit Diesel engine at rear driving through Allison automatic transmission. Other power trains and air-conditioning available. This model has full air suspension. Capacity 49–53 passengers.
23C: **FN** Model TBVI Trolleybus of 1953, one of a fleet of 100-seaters operated in the Liège, Belgium, area and produced by the Fabrique Nationale Herstal SA in nearby Herstal. Note the peculiar windscreen layout.
23D: **Foden** 37-seater Plaxton 'Crusader' coach of 1951. At this time Fodens Ltd of Elworth Works, Sandbach, Cheshire, offered three passenger chassis, viz. the 17 ft 6 in WB PVSC6, the 16 ft 3 in WB PVD6 and a rear-engined chassis with 19 ft 6 in WB. All had a 112-bhp 8·4-litre six-cylinder diesel engine with choice of four- or five-speed gearbox. For the home market the Foden two-stroke 4·1-litre 126-bhp diesel was available.

23A Flxible 'Flxiliner'

23B Flxible 40-ft Transit Coach

23C FN TBVI

23D Foden/Plaxton 'Crusader'

FORD

24A Ford 'Thames'

24B Ford 'Transit'

24C Ford 'Transit'

24A: **Ford** of Britain produced their 400E Series of 10/12- and 15-cwt vans from 1957 until 1965. They featured independent front suspension and a 1703-cc four-cylinder OHV engine (as 'Consul' car). A Perkins diesel was available from 1961. In Sept. 1958 the 402E 12-seater 'mini-bus' appeared as a derivation from the 15-cwt van.
24B: **Ford** 'Transit' vehicles have been produced by the Ford companies in Britain and Germany since 1965, and are available in a variety of bodystyles including this 9-seater bus (Germany: FT900, 1969 model shown; Britain: V20).
24C **Ford** of Britain 'Transit' 9-seater 'Custom' bus of the 1970 18-cwt V20 range with 106-in WB and single rear wheels. Standard engine was 1·7-litre V4 petrol unit which also powered the Ford 'Corsair' car. A 2-litre V4 and a Perkins diesel were also available. At this time there were about 600 possible variations in the 'Transit' range.
24D: **Ford** 'Transit' LWB 175 chassis with Ford 2·4-litre diesel engine and 16-seat municipal bus body by Strachans of Hamble, Hants. Used by London Transport since the autumn of 1972 on routes considered impracticable for conventional bus operation, areas served being Brixton–Dulwich, Bromley Kent, Cricklewood–Archway and Enfield–Southgate. The routes maintain community links for hospitals, welfare centres and off-peak shopping schedules. A feature of the single-fare rate is that, traffic permitting, the buses will stop on demand.

24D Ford/Strachans 'Pacemaker'

FORD (SON)

25A Ford FK3500

25D Ford 'Thames Trader'

25E Ford/Burlingham 'Seagull'

25B Fordson/Lambourn 'Thames'

25C Ford

25A: **Ford**-Köln (Cologne) produced trucks with the American 1940-pattern front end throughout the war and until about 1950, when 'facelifting' of the grille and re-location of the headlights took place. Many were used by the Allied occupation forces in West Germany, with a variety of bodystyles. Shown is an ex-RAF crew coach, now used in Belgium as a personnel carrier.
25B: **Fordson** 'Thames' ET6 V8-engined chassis were produced by Ford of England, during 1949–57, and some were fitted with passenger bodywork. In late 1952 'Fordson' was deleted from the radiator grille badge and 'Thames' became the marque name. The same Briggs Motor Bodies front end, with slight modifications, was utilized by Guy Motors in 1953/54 on 84 'Vixen' 26-seater buses for London Transport.
25C: **Ford** bus chassis of Canadian origin, fitted with British Perkins P6 diesel engine and Indian bodywork, in service with the Bombay State Transport Corporation in the 1950s.
25D: **Ford** 'Thames Trader' 40, Model 609E, truck chassis with bus bodywork for the US Air Force in Great Britain. Also with integral front end (Marshall, Mulliners, 1960/61).
25E: **Ford** 'Thames' 212-inch wheelbase PSV chassis with 'Seagull Sixtyone' 41-seater luxury coach bodywork, introduced by H. V. Burlingham Ltd of Blackpool for the 1961 selling season. It measured 30 ft by 8 ft and had a clerestory type roof with full-length peach opaque perspex panels.

FORD

26A Ford/Harrington 'Crusader'

26B Ford/Duple 'Viceroy' 37

26C Ford/Alexander

26A: **Ford** 'Thames' PSV chassis (petrol: 568E, diesel: 570E) with 41-seat 'Crusader' Mark II luxury coachwork by Thomas Harrington Ltd of Hove, Sussex. This was a 30 × 8 ft body, weighing $2\frac{1}{2}$ tons, made mainly of metal but utilizing plastic fibre-glass panels for the front, front canopy, rear dome, rear lower panels and wheel arches.

26B: **Ford** R-Series 37-ft chassis with 53-seat luxury coach body by the Duple Group. Introduced in late 1968 as an entirely new design and claimed to be the most luxurious coach body in Europe.

26C: By 1972 over thirty **Ford** R-Series single-deck buses were in operation with Alexander Northern of Aberdeen, members of the Scottish Bus Group. The 53-seaters on Model R1114 chassis were bodied by Messrs Walter Alexander & Co (Coachbuilders) Ltd of Falkirk. All Ford R-Series bus chassis have PAS, air-over-hydraulic service brakes and air-operated parking brake.

26D: **Ford** R-Series, Model R114, with 6-litre 'Turbo' diesel and SCG five-speed semi-automatic gearbox. The 49-seat 'Panorama Elite' coachwork was produced by Plaxtons of Scarborough for the City of Coventry Corporation's private hire fleet in 1972.

26D Ford/Plaxton 'Panorama Elite'

27 GMC Buses and Coaches of the Twenties, Thirties and Sixties

"SOLDIERS THREE" — ALL GMC

❶ ARMY TRUCKS

❷ ARMY COACHES

❸ COMMERCIAL TRUCKS

GMC has not one, but *three different products* which are serving with our soldiers in Camps and Forts and Flying Fields across the country. GMC military trucks, by the thousands, are performing numerous transport tasks so vital to the modern army. GMC-built Yellow coaches, in ever increasing quantity, are carrying workers to their war jobs and troops to their war duties. GMC commercial trucks are transporting much of the huge supply of food and equipment required by our rapidly expanding armed forces. "Soldiers Three"... all GMC...these trucks and coaches are helping to make our army the greatest motorized military force in all the world.

Better serviced trucks serve America better! Investigate "Victory Maintenance"—GMC's answer to war-time needs for peak performance, economy and longer truck life. It is available for trucks of all makes through GMC Branches and Dealers everywhere.

GMC VICTORY MAINTENANCE

GENERAL MOTORS TRUCK & COACH

DIVISION OF YELLOW TRUCK & COACH MANUFACTURING COMPANY—HOME OF GMC TRUCKS AND YELLOW COACHES · MANUFACTURER OF A WIDE VARIETY OF MILITARY VEHICLES FOR OUR ARMED FORCES

28A GMC

28A: **GMC** wartime advertisement, highlighting the three main products of 'The Truck People from General Motors' in 1941/42.
28B: **GMC** $2\frac{1}{2}$-ton 6 × 6 trucks were produced in very large numbers throughout World War II, with a variety of bodystyles. After the war the variety became greater still, and even buses were based on this ubiquitous chassis, notably in Germany. The bus illustrated was in service with the Austrian Army in the late Fifties.
28C: **GMC** 41-passenger intercity coach of 1961. Designated PD-4106, it was powered by a 272-bhp General Motors V8 diesel, mounted transversally at the rear. It was equipped with air-conditioning.

28B GMC CCKW-353

28C GMC PD-4106

29A GMC T8H-5307A

29A: **GMC** T8H-5307A city service bus of the early Seventies. It has accommodation for 53 passengers and is powered by a GM Detroit Diesel V8 engine, located transversally at the rear. Entrance is at front (marked: 'Exact fare required—Driver has NO change'), exit in centre.
29B: **GMC** P8M-4905A intercity coach, also known as parlor coach, equipped with air-conditioning, rest room and other conveniences. The vehicle has 47 seats and room for 16 standing passengers, and was delivered to Pine Hill Kingston Bus Corporation in 1972. Like most GMC buses and coaches, it has a rear-mounted Detroit Diesel power unit.
29C: **GMC** Rapid Transit Experimental (RTX) Coach was a design exercise of the late 1960s. The styling of the 40-ft body was not unlike current European designs, with very large windows, and was a breakaway from the aircraft-type styling of most American buses and coaches. Propulsion was by gas turbine.

29B GMC P8M-4905A

29C GMC RTX

GREYHOUND, GUY

30A Greyhound 'Scenicruiser'

30B Guy/ELC 'Wulfrunian'

30A: **Greyhound** Corporation, the famous American passenger transit organization, was formed in 1930 although the individual companies from which it was developed were much older. The name 'Greyhound' was first used for a bus in 1921, by Frank Fageol, a leading American bus builder. Typical of Greyhound buses of the Sixties were standard production GMCs and their own 'Scenicruiser', built by GMC to Greyhound's design. They were introduced in 1954, but were supplemented by the six-wheeled 'Super Scenicruiser' a few years later. They have rear-mounted diesel engines, automatic transmission, air-conditioning, etc. Greyhound Corporation later acquired their own bus factory: Motor Coach Industries Ltd of Winnipeg, Canada and Pembina, North Dakota.

30B: **Guy** 1961 'Wulfrunian' double-decker for Wolverhampton Corporation Transport. Wheelbase was extended to 18 ft (from 15 ft 4 in) and cam-operated drum brakes replaced the standard disc type. A feature of the £3500 chassis was the use of full air suspension. The forward-entrance bodywork was by East Lancashire Coachbuilders Ltd and provided accommodation for 72 passengers.

30C: **Guy** 'Victory' LHD chassis with Leyland 680 150-bhp 11·1-litre six-cylinder underfloor diesel engine and 46-seater long-distance touring coach bodywork by the Belgian firm of Jonckheere, for Ostendia Cars, Ostend. Specification included adjustable aircraft-type seats and, at the rear, a toilet compartment, and a small galley with hot and cold water. 1962.

30C Guy/Jonckheere 'Victory'

31A: **Hino** RC320P coach, one of the products of Hino Motors Ltd of Tokyo, Japan. It provides luxury accommodation for 55 passengers and weighs 8085 kg. The rear-mounted 10·2-litre 200-bhp six-cylinder underfloor diesel engine drives through a five-speed gearbox, providing a maximum speed of 91 km/h. 1970.

31B: **Ikarus** is the name of Hungary's national passenger vehicle production enterprise formed in 1949, but with origins going back to 1895. Several types are made, including articulated. In addition to integral types there are coaches on imported Steyr and Volvo chassis. Shown is a 12-metre 30 + 3-seater 250SL luxury coach of 1971/72 with Rába-MAN six-cylinder diesel, air suspension, air-conditioning and other modern features.

31C: This remarkable double-deck 117-seater semi-trailer type bus was operated by Santa Fé Trailways in the USA during World War II. The tractor unit, derived from the International D500 COE truck, had a wheelbase of a mere 74 inches and was only the propulsion/steering unit, the driver sitting in the passenger compartment.

31D: **International** 'Loadstar' school bus chassis of 1969 with RHD, and body with left-hand side entrance/exit doors for use by US Air Force in Great Britain. Power unit was an International 193-bhp petrol/gasoline OHV V-8-cylinder, driving through a five-speed manual gearbox.

31A Hino RC320P

31B Ikarus 250SL

31C International/Santa Fé

31D International 'Loadstar'

KAROSA, KARRIER

32A: **Karosa** SD11 42-seater, produced in Czechoslovakia to modern European design with integral body construction, air suspension, twin-circuit air brakes and six-cylinder 180-bhp Skoda ML630 underfloor diesel engine mounted amidships, driving through a five-speed gearbox. The 11-metres long vehicle is shown with a four-wheel trailer, a not unusual combination in its home country. 1970.
32B: Towards the end of 1960 Jersey Motor Transport Co Ltd took over the Promenade Bus Service and, with it, two **Karrier** 'Bantam'-based open 25-seaters, produced originally in 1948. These were taken into service after the engines and chassis had been reconditioned and the bodies completely rebuilt. As can be seen, the bodywork was of simple and completely open design without provision for weatherproofing.
32C: **Karrier** 14-seater coach drawn alongside Lord Nelson's Flagship *Victory* at Portsmouth, 1953.

32B Karrier 'Bantam'

32A Karosa SD11

32C Karrier

33A Karrier 'Gamecock' Mk II

33C Karrier/Lauber

33B Karrier BFD 3023

33A: These two unusual but attractive-looking coaches were built in South Africa, in 1958, on diesel-engined **Karrier** 'Gamecock' chassis. They were specially equipped for a 20,000-mile trip from Johannesburg to Europe, visiting 17 countries. The 11 ft 9 in WB chassis were powered by the Rootes TS3 two-stroke diesel engine which was available from September 1954 to August 1958, when it was superseded by the Rootes C305 six-cylinder diesel. In March 1959 the TS3 became available again, in addition to the C305 and the underfloor petrol six-cylinder, which was standard.
33B: **Karrier** 10 ft 3 in WB diesel-engined chassis with special 14-seater coach bodywork by Reading & Co Ltd of Portsmouth. Built to the order of Rootes Ltd (Export Division) in the late Fifties, the vehicle was supplied to the Ashanti Goldfields Corporation Ltd in Ghana. The body was of light alloy construction, fully insulated and fitted with Airvac roof vents. This chassis was usually supplied under the Commer name.
33C: **Karrier** components were used in some luxury coaches built in 1960/61 by Lauber & Fils of Nyon, Switzerland, for Voyages Louis, Nyon (shown), Autobus Lausannois, and Escursions Leyvraz, Aigle. They were powered by Rootes TS3 diesel engines mounted at the rear. There were 22-, 26-(shown) and 30-seaters. Except for the 22-seater, they had four-speed synchromesh gearboxes with air pressure/electrically-assisted gear change and Eaton two-speed axles.

KÄSSBOHRER

34A : **Kässbohrer** is an old-established German coachbuilding firm, whose first bus body appeared in 1911. Exactly forty years later came the first 'Setra' chassis-less coach. (Setra was derived from *selbsttragend*, German for self-supporting.) Illustrated is a 1964 Model S125 10·65-metre city bus with rear-mounted Henschel 150-bhp diesel engine. It could carry up to 125 passengers, 34 seated and 91 standing.

34B : **Kässbohrer** Setra S124 46-seat luxury coach built in 1966 for a Swiss customer and claimed to be the longest coach available, with a width not exceeding 2·30 metres. The rear-mounted 172-bhp Henschel diesel drove through an eight-speed ZF gearbox.

34C : **Kässbohrer** Setra S150, the company's largest two-axle coach of the late Sixties and early Seventies. It could have up to 15 seat rows, or 55 to 63 seats. Overall length was 12 metres. The 230-bhp diesel drove through a ZF six-speed overdrive gearbox.

34D : **Kässbohrer** Super-Setra 40-ft 'Silver Eagle', one of some 200 long-distance coaches supplied to Continental Trailways of Dallas, Texas, during 1956–61 for trans-continental use in the USA.

34E : **Kässbohrer** Super-Setra articulated coach, also in service with Continental Trailways in the USA. The firm's standard articulated buses, Model SG175, were first introduced in 1953 and accommodated up to 175 persons. They had three axles, air suspension and Büssing or Henschel underfloor diesel engines.

34B Kässbohrer Setra S12A

34A Kässbohrer Setra S125

34C Kässbohrer Setra S150

34D Kässbohrer Super-Setra 'Silver Eagle'

34E Kässbohrer Super-Setra 'Golden Eagle'

35A Leyland/DAB 'Leopard'

35B Leyland 'Comet'

35C Leyland/Park Royal 'Panther'

35D Leyland/Caetano 'Leopard'

35A: **Leyland** two-entrance 42-seat 36-ft luxury coach, bodied by Dansk Automobil Byggeri AS of Silkeborg, Denmark, in 1962 on Model PSU3/4L chassis for an Israeli operator. The coach embodied a cocktail bar, toilet and washroom, and was powered by a 130-bhp Leyland 0·600 horizontal diesel, with four-speed 'Pneumo-Cyclic' gearbox.
35B: **Leyland** 'Comet' chassis with passenger bodywork by Martins & Caetano Lda of Oporto, Portugal, for Expresso do Viga Lda in Angola, awaiting fitment of cargo body to rear of chassis. Three of these unusual vehicles were supplied in the mid-Sixties.
35C: **Leyland** 'Panther' PSUR1/1L chassis with 39-seat Park Royal bodywork, one of a £$2\frac{1}{2}$m. fleet of buses ordered by Stockholm Tramways for delivery in 1967. The 160-bhp horizontal Leyland 0·680 diesel was located under the floor at rear. Chassis price was £3853.
35D: **Leyland** 'Leopard' bus/coach chassis for 12-metre bodywork. Shown with Portuguese luxury air-conditioned coach body. Underfloor engines up to 200 bhp, and four- or five-speed manual or semi-auto. trans. were available. 1970.

LEYLAND

36A: **Leyland** mechanical components and Dutch **Verheul** integral bodywork formed this French-operated rear-engined country bus of 1969/70.
36B: 'Midi-Bus' body, specially designed for the **Leyland** 'Terrier' TR950 chassis, as produced by Leyland Motors (Scotland) Ltd in Bathgate, West Lothian, under the Leyland Redline name. The body was made by J. H. Sparshatt & Sons Ltd of Portsmouth (now part of the Wadham Stringer Group). Available as 30-seater or as school bus for 40 children. 1972.
36C: Prototype o-m-o dual entrance/exit bus announced by the **Leyland National** Company Ltd, which was founded in 1969 with the specific purpose of producing passenger vehicles jointly by British Leyland and the National Bus Company. Production started in 1971/72 in a new plant at Lilliehall, Workington, Cumberland.
36D: 1972 production-model of the **Leyland National**. Specification includes a 180- or 200-bhp rear-mounted Leyland 510 fixed-head horizontal six-cylinder diesel, fluid coupling with lock-up clutch, 4- or 5-speed semi- or fully-automatic gearbox, double-reduction rear axle, I-beam front axle, rolling lobe air suspension of the low-frequency type with self-levelling geometry, power-assisted rack and pinion steering gear mounted on the axle and full air dual-circuit brakes. Overall length 10·3 or 11·3 metres.

36B Leyland Redline/Sparshatt

36C Leyland National

36D Leyland National

36A Leyland/Verheul LV45

37A Leyland PD2/1

37A: Ex-London Transport 'RTL'-Type **Leyland** double-decker of 1949 vintage in New York. Note the changed frontal appearance caused by the additional bumper and radiator guard.

37B: **Leyland** 'Titan' PD2/20 with 59-seat rear-entrance body by East Lancs. Delivered in 1955 to Rawtenstall Corporation, which later became Rossendale Corporation.

37C: **Leyland** introduced their rear-engined 'Atlantean' in 1958. A modification, Model PDR1/2, was announced in 1964. It had a new dropped-centre rear axle, allowing a low, continuous level floor in the lower saloon. The engine was a rear-mounted vertical Leyland 0·600 9·8-litre 130-bhp diesel. Re-disposition of the drive line enabled the 'Pneumo-Cyclic' gearbox and/or angle-drive unit to be removed without disturbing engine and radiator. This was one of 21 for Sheffield Corporation.

37D: One of fifteen **Leyland** 'Atlantean' 77-seaters supplied in 1971 to Plymouth. The specification included air-operated doors, Videmat ticket machines, Formica finished ceilings, domes, sides and seat backs, tread-operated passenger counting device and Leyland 0·680 11·1-litre rear-mounted diesel engine. This batch brought the total of Plymouth City Transport's fleet of rear-engined double-deckers to 158, all based on the 'Atlantean' chassis.

37B Leyland/East Lancs. 'Titan'

37C Leyland/Park Royal 'Atlantean'

37D Leyland/Park Royal 'Atlantean'

38A Magirus O330a

38B Magirus-Deutz O3500

38C Magirus-Deutz 'Saturn II'

38D Magirus-Deutz 150L10

38A: During World War II **Magirus** production was concentrated on three-ton trucks with 4 × 2 and 4 × 4 drive. Variants were the O3300 and O330a two- and four-wheel drive buses. In 1942 a fleet of the latter was supplied to the Transport Ministry in Pressburg (German name of Bratislava, Czechoslovakia). Instead of the familiar Magirus emblem, these sported a circular Klöckner-Deutz sign, but no emblem at all was carried on an austere version (*Primitivausführung*).

38B: In 1951 the Ulm plant of Klöckner-Humboldt-Deutz introduced new **Magirus-Deutz** normal-control chassis. They were powered by Deutz air-cooled four- and six-cylinder diesels. This successful range with *Haifisch-Schnauze* (shark snout) was continued for many years. The bus chassis, however, was dropped in 1953.

38C: 'Saturn II' was the name for a new generation of **Magirus-Deutz** coaches and buses. Illustrated is a luxury touring coach with slanted window pillars, first announced at Nizza in 1960. In 1956 Magirus bus production had been transferred to the KHD plant at Mainz-Mombach, and the 'Saturn II' was the first new type to emerge from there. It was of semi-integral construction, incorporating a sub-frame carrying the air suspension and axle units.

38D: **Magirus-Deutz** 'Special'. The Frankfurt fire brigade acquired this vehicle in 1968 for use as a command post. It is equipped with radio, communication, microfilm and other equipment.

39A: **Magirus-Deutz** 28-seater (*Kleinbus*), introduced at the 1969 Frankfurt Motor Show, together with the 33-seat 120L80. Both had a length of 7·40 metres and 3·65-metre WB. Parabola-type springs are used at front and rear. The 120R80 is intended for touring coach purposes, the 120L80 for use as personnel transporter and school bus, the former having luxury travel seats with separate back rests. Both have a rear-mounted 120-bhp air-cooled Deutz diesel engine.

39B: **MAN** Diesel tractive unit with double cab and city bus semi-trailer built in 1943 for the city of Kiel, Germany. The bodywork was by Karl Kässbohrer and the vehicle was propelled by gas, carried in a 50-cubic metre balloon located in the roof.

39C: The **MAN** 760U01 was introduced in the late Fifties and was of integral construction. The engine was a horizontal 8·7-litre 160-bhp six-cylinder diesel (MAN D1546M1U) mounted between the axles and accessible from the left-hand side. A six-speed synchromesh gearbox was standard, but both ZF-Hydromedia and Voith-Diwabus automatic transmissions were available. Overall length was 11·3 metres, WB 5·65. Carrying capacity was 31 seated passengers and 93 standees.

39D: Rear-engined lightweight coach with **MAN** mechanical components (incl. 135-bhp 'M'-diesel engine) and **Krauss-Maffei** bodywork, produced in 1959.

39A Magirus-Deutz 120R80

39C MAN 760U01

39B MAN/Kässbohrer

39D MAN/Krauss-Maffei KMS135

40A MAN 760UO2G

40B MAN 750HO-M11A

40A: **MAN** 760UO2G *Gelenkbus*. This articulated bus was in service with the city of Augsburg, about 1960. The construction of the vehicle was generally similar to that of other German articulated buses, such as Büssing (now merged with MAN), Daimler-Benz and Kässbohrer.
40B: **MAN** Metrobus 'undercarriage' on display. Main features: 160-bhp direct-injection rear-mounted underfloor engine, independent front suspension, rear axle with separate carrying and driving components, air springing, dual-circuit brakes (front: air-hyd., rear: air), GVW 15,000 kg. 1969/70.
40C: This electric bus was designed and produced by **MAN** of Munich in co-operation with Bosch of Stuttgart, RWE of Essen and Varta of Frankfurt, in 1970/71, as a contribution from the industry to combat air pollution and noise in city traffic. It was designed in such a way that it could be used on city routes; after tests by the manufacturers it was taken into service in Koblenz, Germany. The heavy batteries, still the major obstacle in electrically propelled vehicles, are carried in a one-axle trailer and give a radius of action of about 50 km, after which they are exchanged for freshly charged units. Bus and trailer are 10 + 2·9 metres long and together, including batteries, weigh 13,100 kg. The motor has an output of 108 kW (147 hp) and the maximum speed is about 60 km/h.

40C MAN Elektro-Bus

41A: Now all but forgotten, the **Maudslay** Motor Co Ltd of Alcester, Warwickshire, offered several types of passenger vehicle chassis during the 1940s. In 1948 the following chassis were listed: 'Marathon' II (32–39-seater, WB 17 ft 7 in, 120-bhp petrol engine), 'Marathon' III (as II but 98-bhp 7·7-litre diesel) and 'Marathon' LH (export chassis with 125-bhp 9·6-litre diesel engine and 17 ft 7 in or 20 ft WB). All engines had six cylinders and drove through five-speed constant-mesh gearboxes, with the exception of the 'Marathon' III which had four speeds. The 'Marathon' III illustrated was supplied to Blakes, a Cornish customer. It was bodied by Whitson and weighed $6\frac{1}{2}$ tons. James Whitson & Co Ltd of Sipson, West Drayton, Middx, built bus bodies of several types on Maudslay, Austin, Commer, Dennis and other chassis, and later specialized in fibre-glass bodies and components.

41B: **Maudslay** 'Marathon' Mark III chassis with half-cab coach bodywork by Plaxtons (Scarborough) Ltd, produced about 1950. In 1948 Maudslay had become a member of the ACV Group (Associated Commercial Vehicles), together with AEC and Crossley. The Maudslay name ceased to exist as a vehicle make in 1960.

41A Maudslay 'Marathon' III

41B Maudslay 'Marathon' III

MERCEDES-BENZ

42A Mercedes-Benz O319

42B Mercedes-Benz O321H

42C Mercedes-Benz O317

42D Mercedes-Benz O309

42A: The **Mercedes-Benz** O319 bus, with up to 18 seats, was introduced in the mid-Fifties and was a factory-supplied modification of the L319 van. It had a four-cylinder 65-bhp petrol engine, but the diesel engine of the contemporary Mercedes-Benz 180D car was available at extra cost. The diesel developed 43 bhp and buses thus equipped were designated O319D. The basic version of 1955, which had 17 seats, is shown. There was also a luxury type with 10 individual seats and an 18-seater personnel carrier.
42B: The **Mercedes-Benz** O321H was introduced in 1954, and by the end of the Fifties more than 9000 had been produced. It was designed at a time when buses and coaches generally became purpose-built vehicles rather than derivatives of truck chassis. The O321H was of integral construction with subframe, rear-mounted six-cylinder 120-bhp diesel engine, fully-synchronized five-speed gearbox and three separate brake systems. Depending on interior layout, it had 37 to 47 luxury seats in the touring coach (shown) and up to 70 seats in the city bus version.
42C: The **Mercedes-Benz** O317 120-passenger city bus made its debut in 1957 as Germany's first bus with air suspension. The engine, mounted under the floor, was a six-cylinder diesel of 220 SAE-bhp, driving through a conventional or hydraulic transmission. Illustrated is a 1960 production model.
42D: **Mercedes-Benz** O309 is the bus version of the contemporary forward-control panel van, available with petrol or diesel engine (O309B and O309D resp.), both with either 2·95- or 3·50-metre WB. There were several options as regards door and seating arrangements. 1966.

43A Mercedes-Benz O302

43C Mercedes-Benz O305

43B Mercedes-Benz O302

43A: **Mercedes-Benz** O302 models, city bus, country bus and coach, were introduced in 1965. They were of the rear-engined integral type with either steel or air suspension. An early model is shown. Note the high curved side windows.

43B: **Mercedes-Benz** O302 of 1968. This particular coach was the 5000th produced, and featured many improvements over the earlier ones. It had a 255-SAE-hp engine and was supplied to Washington, USA, for sightseeing tours, after having been exhibited at the Swiss Motor Show in Geneva.

43C: This modern **Mercedes-Benz** standard city service bus with low floor has an overall length of 11 metres, a wheelbase of 5·60 metres and capacity for up to 85 sitting and standing passengers. The bus is powered by a 170-DIN-bhp Daimler-Benz OM360h six-cylinder diesel, mounted at the rear and driving through a manual synchromesh ZF gearbox. Diwabus automatic transmission is available. The body is of integral construction and air-suspended on rigid axles. The brake system is of the twin-circuit air type, the steering hydraulically assisted. Note the wide entrance and exit doors which are both of the double-leaf type. The bus was designed in 1967 to comply with the VÖV specification (Association of Public Transport Services) of which some 170 operators are members. The main object of the 'VÖV'-standard city bus was, and is, rational production, and hence a reasonable purchase price and a decrease in maintenance costs by means of simplified maintenance.

MCW, MITSUBISHI, NEOPLAN

44A MCW 'Metro-Scania'

44A: Rear-engined o-m-o bus of integral construction produced by **Metro-Cammell-Weymann** Ltd in Washwood Heath, Birmingham, England, utilizing Swedish mechanical components from Scania Bussar, the bus division of Saab-Scania. This bus was built for Leicester City Transport in 1970 and has 44 seats, double-glazing, PAS, air suspension auto. trans. and other refinements. In 1972 a fully-integral double-decker was introduced.
44B: **Mitsubishi** Heavy Industries Ltd of Tokyo, Japan, produce a variety of passenger vehicles. That shown is a 10·66-metre 45-seater with rear-mounted 8·5-litre diesel engine, operated in Singapore (mid-1960s).
44C: **Neoplan** NH10 9·10-metre 38-seater, one of a range produced by Karosserie-und Fahrzeugbau Gottlob Auwärter KG of Stuttgart-Möhringen in the late 1960s. Seating arrangements were available for 35 to 43. The engine was at the rear and drove through a five-speed gearbox. Similar but longer models were designated NH12 (43–51 seats) and NH16 (51–59). There were also two shorter models, the NH6 (18–27) and NH8 (27–35).
44D: **Neoplan** 12-metre double-deck coach, available with up to 105 seats. This attractive three-axle model was offered, with various power trains, for motorway speeds of up to 120 km/h. 1972.

44B Mitsubishi Fuso R710

44C Neoplan NH10

44D Neoplan NH22/3 'Skyliner'

NEOPLAN, NISSAN, OPEL

45A: In 1966 the **Neoplan** Hotelbus was introduced as the first of its type in the world. The lower deck provides 30 seats and the upper deck the sleeping accommodation. Also upstairs are two shower cubicles, two toilets and a kitchen. Other features include air-conditioning, radio, record player, television, oil heating, etc. Electric power is provided by a VW engine-driven generating set.
45B: The **Neoplan** 'Intercityliner' is a high-decker with 52 luxury seats. Below the floor are toilet and washing facilities, large luggage compartments, wardrobe, sleeping accommodation for the (co-)driver, etc. Various power trains (up to 320 bhp) are available. 1971/72.
45C: **Nissan** Motor Co Ltd during the mid-1960s offered several types of rear-engined diesel buses, including this Model 4R103 (4RA103 if equipped with air suspension) which offered accommodation for 45 seated persons and 38 standees, plus a crew of 2. If equipped with front instead of centre door, the capacity was 49 + 39 + 2.
45D: **Opel** 'Blitz' bus chassis with Imbert producer gas equipment and Kässbohrer bodywork produced for the Deutsche Reichspost in 1941. The picture was taken in 1941 in Ulm/Donau and on the left shows Otto Kässbohrer, the son of the founder of the Kässbohrer coachbuilding business.

45B Neoplan N116 'Intercityliner'

45C Nissan 4F103

45A Neoplan Hotelbus

45D Opel 'Blitz'

PEGASO

46A Pegaso 'Monocasco'

46A/B: **Pegaso** 'Monocasco' was a luxury observation coach produced in 1950 and featuring chassisless construction. There were two versions, namely the De Luxe with 43 + 2 seats and the 'Pullman' long-distance coach with 34 + 2 seats. Both measured 10·00 × 2·50 × 3·27 metres and the weight was approximately 7700 kg. The 125-bhp vertical six-cylinder Pegaso diesel engine was mounted amidships. A six-cylinder Pegaso petrol engine of 145 to 170 bhp, good for a cruising speed of 100 km/h, was offered alternatively.

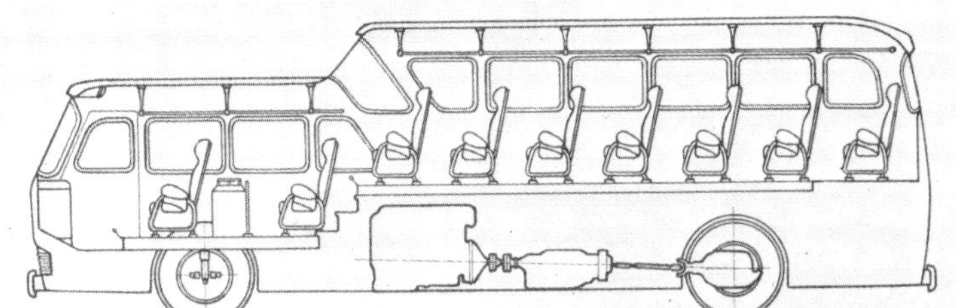

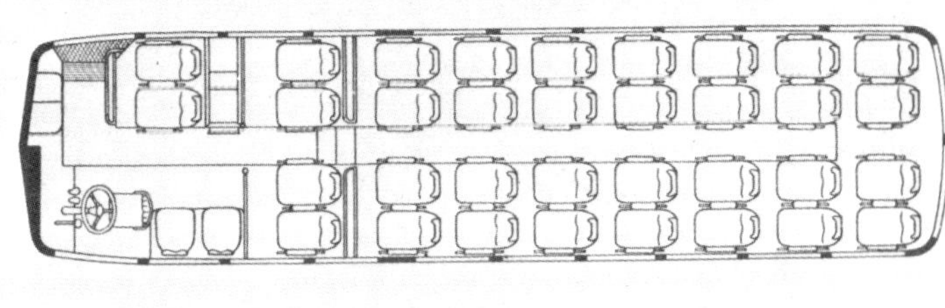

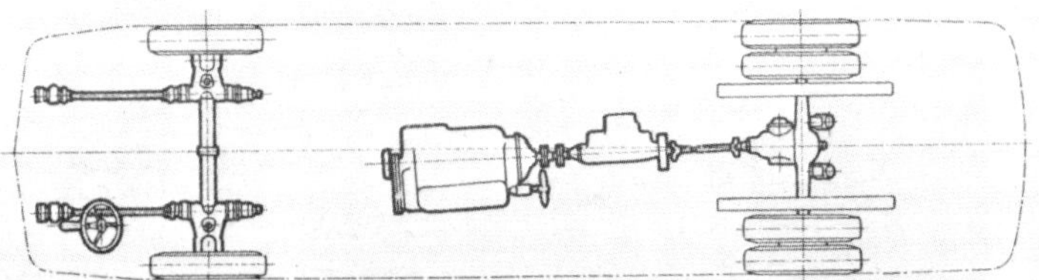

46B Pegaso 'Monocasco'

PEGASO

47A: **Pegaso** Model 6035A of 1967 was an articulated city bus of the same general design as equivalent German types. It was powered by a Leyland diesel engine.
47B: Commercial **Pegaso** SA of Madrid, Spain, in 1968 offered a range of buses and coaches, including the 5031L/1, the 5065DR and the 6030NA. An example of the latter is shown. It had an underfloor six-cylinder diesel engine, mounted within the wheelbase, and single tyres all round. For many years this manufacturer utilized British Leyland engines, axles and other components. It produces a wide range of trucks also.
47C: This air-conditioned luxury coach was exhibited by **Pegaso** at the 1971 Paris Motor Show. It has a rear-mounted 170-bhp Pegaso six-cylinder diesel engine with a cubic capacity of 10,170 cc, driving through a six-speed synchromesh gearbox. The gross vehicle weight is 12,000 kg. The coach has luxury seating for 33 + 1 passengers.

47B Pegaso 6030NA

47A Pegaso 6035A

47C Pegaso 6046

REO, ROBUR, SAURER

48A Reo 'M-Series'

48B Robur LO2500

48C Saurer 3DH

48A: **Reo** $2\frac{1}{2}$-ton 6 × 6 US military truck chassis of the Fifties, bodied by the Greek firm of Tangalakis. In all probability this vehicle started life as an M35 cargo truck (M34 had single rear tyres) before being converted for use by the Greek Air Force. The bodywork follows the styling of the US 'school bus' type.

48B: **Robur** LO2500 truck chassis of East German manufacture, with special passenger bodywork, used by the Czech state-owned transport firm ČSAD to carry passengers to and from the 14th-century Karlštejn Castle, not far from Prague. 1968.

48C: The **Saurer** 3DH for 39–43 passengers was developed in 1960/61, by Saurer and the Association of the Swiss Coachbuilding Industry (VSCI). Bodies were built by various coachbuilders to a common general specification. It had a rear-mounted Saurer CT4DLm 6·8-litre 150-bhp vertical six-cylinder diesel, driving through an eight-speed gearbox (four-speed + overdrive). Wheelbase was 5·2, overall length 10·7 metres.

49A Saviem/Chausson APH

49C Saviem SC2

49B Saviem/Chausson APVU

49D Saviem SC5

49A: Forty-five-seater **Saviem/Chausson** APH inter-city bus with conventionally-mounted four-cylinder diesel engine. During the Fifties the Model APH was produced by SA des Usines Chausson of Asnières. In 1960 Chausson was absorbed in the Saviem combine, which already comprised Somua, Latil, Floirat, Isobloc, and the truck and bus division of Renault. The Chausson name was continued until the Saviem name eventually ousted all the individual marque names. Similar in appearance to the APH were the six-cylinder models AHH and ASH. All had 5·12-metre WB and 14·5-ton GVW rating.
49B: **Saviem/Chausson** 'bus urban' (urban bus) of the early Sixties. It had a front-mounted diesel engine, front entrance and centre exit. The single rear tyres were a Chausson feature dating back to the 1940s.
49C: **Saviem** SC2 long-distance coach featured 45 comfortable seats, observation windows in the roof sides and, like the Saviem/Chausson APH, a long roof luggage rack. Similar in appearance was the SC1, which, in addition, had observation windows above the windscreen.
49D: The **Saviem** SC5 was a medium-sized tourist coach with seating for 31 to 37 passengers, depending on interior layout. It was introduced in 1961.

SAVIEM

50A Saviem S45

50B Saviem SC10

50C Saviem E7N

50A: Series-produced **Saviem** 45-passenger service bus introduced in 1966. Specimen shown was operated by French Army; same type was also used by French Air Force and Navy. It was powered by a MAN 150-bhp six-cylinder diesel engine, driving through a six-speed manual gearbox. Air-actuated service brakes were standard, as were Michelin E20X tyres, single all round. Overall dimensions: 10·62 × 2·50 × 2·82 metres. Net weight 7800 kg, GVW 14,500 kg.

50B: The **Saviem** SC10 is a standard city bus and is in service in considerable numbers throughout France. A similar bus is produced by Berliet (Model PCM). On the SC10 the engine is located under the floor at the forward end.

50C: **Saviem** E7N luxury coach, introduced at the 1970 Paris Motor Show. This is a 10·5-metre model with 45 seats. Also available is a 12-metre model with 53 seats. Both have a large underfloor luggage compartment and a rear-mounted 235-bhp MAN 10·35-litre vertical six-cylinder diesel engine.

50D: In the late 1950s **Renault** produced this city bus in several versions. A three-door model for two-man operation is shown. It had a 5·58-metre WB and was 10·8 metres long. The diesel engine was mounted amidships, under the floor. The conductor had his own 'box office', by the rear door. There was room for 22 seated passengers and a large number of standees.

50D Saviem-LRS-Renault 4192

51A: **Scania-Vabis** rear-engined city bus of the early Fifties. Doors (front entrance, rear exit) were of the double two-leaf folding type. Note the sharp angle of the front wheels, shown at full lock. At this time the Swedes still drove on the left-hand side of the road.
51B: In 1948/49 **Seddon** Motors Ltd of Oldham, Lancashire, offered one passenger chassis, the Mk 4 for 32-seat bodywork. It had a 14 ft 11 in WB and weighed 2 tons $16\frac{1}{2}$ cwt (2870 kg). The GVW was 6 tons 15 cwt. Power was provided by a Perkins P6 six-cylinder 70-bhp diesel, driving through a five-speed constant-mesh gearbox. The hydro-mechanical service brakes were servo-assisted. The specimen shown has 'full-fronted' bodywork by Barnards of Norwich and was supplied to G. W. Willings of Burton-upon-Trent, Staffordshire. In the early Fifties a 16 ft 4 in WB chassis (Mk 6) was introduced for 35-seat bodies.
51C: **Seddon** Mk 4 with the maker's own coachwork of about 1950. The panelling was in aluminium and is shown unpainted. The design featured a 'tin front' bolt-on grille, rather than the standard Seddon radiator grille of the other coaches shown here.
51D: **Seddon** Mk 4 LHD chassis with typical Belgian 36-passenger coachwork, supplied about 1952 through Ets Hocke in Brussels to Cosmopolite Cars of the same city. It featured a full panel sliding roof and retained the classic Seddon radiator. In the background is the Leopold I Memorial at Brussels.

51C Seddon Mark 4

51A Scania-Vabis

51B Seddon Mark 4

51D Seddon Mark 4

SEDDON

52A Seddon 'PennineRU'

52B Seddon 'Pennine RU'

52C Seddon/Plaxton 'Panorama Elite II'

52A: **Seddon** passenger vehicles of the late Sixties were purpose-built rather than derived from current truck chassis. The 'Pennine RU' of 1969/70 had a rear-mounted 10·45-litre Gardner 6HLX diesel engine of 150 bhp, and was designed as a complete integral unit with the main outrigger frame assembly acting as chassis and body floor frame. It was constructed to qualify for the MoT's grant scheme for stage carriage vehicles. Two WB sizes were offered, 5·03 metres for 10·19-metre bodywork (shown) and 5·64 metres for 11-metre bodywork. The gearbox was an SCG four-speed semi-automatic. Bodywork for this bus, for Doncaster Corporation Transport, was produced by Seddon Motors' Bus and Coach Division.

52B: **Seddon** 'Pennine RU' in the livery of Lancashire United Transport Ltd. Note the two-leaf doors with large glass area. Crosville of Chester also acquired 'Pennine RU' buses.

52C: The **Seddon** 'Pennine IV' chassis is powered by a six- or eight-cylinder diesel engine (120-bhp 5·8-litre Perkins 6·354 or 179-bhp 8·36-litre Perkins V8·510), driving through a five-speed gearbox. A two-speed rear axle is available. Prior to 1970 the 'Pennine IV' was powered by a Deutz diesel (120-bhp F6L912 six-in-line, or 170-bhp F6L413 six-in-Vee). The coach shown was fitted with the Perkins 6·354 and 51-seater luxury body by Plaxtons, who call it the 'Panorama Elite II'. It was supplied to Messrs Hanworth Acorn at London's Heathrow Airport.

52D: **Seddon** 'Pennine IV' 16-ft WB chassis with Perkins 6·354 diesel engine and Seddon-built bus body for one-man operation by the Green Bus Company of Rugeley, Staffordshire.

52D Seddon 'Pennine IV'

53A Skoda 706RTO

53B Sunbeam-BTH 'W'-Type

53C Sunbeam-BTH MF2

53A: **Skoda** 706RTO diesel chassis with bodywork by Karosa, one of a large fleet operated by the Czech transport enterprise ČSAD during the Sixties. The specimen shown was photographed in front of the ancient castle of Kroměříž, Morava. The 706RTO was powered by a six-cylinder 170-bhp Skoda diesel engine, mounted at the front. There were also city bus and touring coach variants.

53B: **Sunbeam-BTH** trolleybus chassis. Typical example of a two-axle 'W'-Type chassis produced by the Sunbeam Moorfield Works at Wolverhampton, jointly for Sunbeam and Karrier. The 'W'-Type chassis was a wartime design prepared by Sunbeam Commercial Vehicles Ltd at the request of the Ministry of War Transport and was suitable for single- or double-deck bodies, the latter for up to approx. 56 passengers.

53C: **Sunbeam-BTH** MF2 trolleybus, one of a fleet supplied to St Helens Corporation Transport Department about 1942. The chassis were originally built for Johannesburg, in South Africa, but were diverted by the Ministry of War Transport for use in Britain. The vehicles had an overall width of 8 ft, which was 6 in wider than normally permitted for public service vehicles in this country.

SUNBEAM, TATRA

54A **Sunbeam-BTH** trolleybus, Model MS2C six-wheeler, one of a number supplied to Rotherham Corporation Transport Department in 1940. This chassis was suitable for double-deck bodies, or large-capacity single-deckers as used by the Rotherham authorities. Note the central entrance/exit doors.
54B: **Tatra** bus on modified Model 27b truck chassis of 1943. An Imbert wood-burning gas producer plant was built in the right rear corner of the bodywork.
54C: **Tatra** 500HB was produced in Czechoslovakia in 1955 for service in mountainous areas. It was a 61-seater with 125-bhp air-cooled V8 diesel engine, mounted at the rear, and driving both rear axles through a four-speed transmission.
54D: **Tatra** 400 trolleybus, one of 125 manufactured in 1947/48. They were 82-seater six-wheelers with a wheelbase of 4·40 + 1·35 metres.

54B Tatra 27bH

54A Sunbeam-BTH MS2C

54C Tatra 500HB

54D Tatra 400

55A Tatra 401

55B Thornycroft SG/NR6

55C Thornycroft 'Sturdy'

55A: **Tatra** 401 trolleybus of the Sixties. It weighed 11,200 kg and had a carrying capacity of 6450 kg. Wheelbase was 4·76 + 1·58 metres, maximum speed 70 km/h. Propulsion was by four 35kW 300V electric motors.
55B: **Thornycroft** half-cab passenger chassis of the late Forties. The model designation SG/NR6 indicated the chassis (Model SG) and the engine, in this case a Model NR6 7·88-litre 100-bhp six-cylinder diesel (the same as in the Thornycroft 'Amazon' WF8/NR6 6 × 4 truck). A chassis under test is shown, accounting for the rather worn rear tyres.
55C: **Thornycroft** 'Sturdy' diesel bus, one of a fleet of 24-seaters operated by Poona Municipality in India. The all-metal bodywork was by General Motors of Bombay.
55D: The use of a truck chassis with passenger bodywork can make for economy in the provision of spare parts and maintenance in a fleet comprising both types. This principle was exemplified by this Park Royal 30-seat contractor's body on a 1950 **Thornycroft** 'Trident' chassis, operated in the Middle East by the IPC. The 'Trident' RHN/CR6 was a 10-ton GVW chassis with 13 ft 6 in WB. The engine, a 5·5-litre CR6 petrol six-cylinder, had an output of 78 bhp at 1900 rpm. Shown alongside it is an American International 'KB'-line truck.

55D Thornycroft 'Trident'

THORNYCROFT, TILLING-STEVENS

56A Thornycroft 'Trident'

56B Thornycroft 'Trident'

56C Tilling-Stevens K6LA7

56A: The **Thornycroft** 'Trident' PG/CR6/1 export chassis differed from the home market model (RG) principally in respect of tyres, suspension and brakes. Basically a forward-control truck chassis, it was frequently used for the mounting of locally-produced bus bodies in several Commonwealth countries, particularly in Africa. It had a 13 ft 6 in WB and was rated for a GVW of 12 tons. The engine was a 90-bhp six-cylinder 5·5-litre diesel (Thornycroft CR6/1), driving through a five-speed or six-speed (with overdrive) gearbox. Brakes were hydraulic with compressed-air servo.
56B: **Thornycroft** 'Trident' export chassis with attractive locally-produced bodywork operated in Australia from the late Fifties.
56C: **Tilling-Stevens** Motors Ltd of Maidstone, Kent, started as manufacturers of petrol-electric buses (W. A. Stevens Ltd) for Thomas Tilling Ltd, bus operators. Until 1930 only petrol-electric trucks and buses were made; afterwards these were joined by conventional types. Eventually the company was absorbed by the Rootes Group, after having merged with Vulcan. In 1948 two passenger chassis were offered: the K6LA7 for 32-seaters, powered by a 102-bhp 8·4-litre six-cylinder diesel and the K5LA7, for 36-seaters, with 85-bhp 7·0-litre five-cylinder diesel. The luxury radio-equipped coach shown was supplied to J. W. Hands, Star Coaches, of Yardley, Birmingham. The bodywork was by James Whitson & Co Ltd of West Drayton, Middx.

TOYOTA, TV

57A Toyota FY

57B Toyota 'Coaster' RU18-H

57A: **Toyota** Model FY bus of 1952. Basically a 4·37-metre wheelbase truck chassis with bus bodywork. Two interior layouts were available: one with longitudinal seats for about 23 seated passengers and centre space for standees, and one with transverse bench seats and centre aisle, seating 29, both including a full-width back seat. In addition there was a forward-control chassis with centre doors. The engine was a 95-bhp 3·8-litre OHV Six, virtually a carbon-copy of the American Chevrolet.

57B: The **Toyota** 'Coaster' was a 25-seater bus with 95-bhp four-cylinder petrol engine of two-litre cubic capacity, although a 70-bhp $2\frac{1}{2}$-litre diesel was available. It was introduced in 1968 and continued until superseded by the RU19-HD of 1972. The latter has a 106-bhp petrol engine.

57C: The **TV** is a product of the Autobuzul Factory of Bucharest, Rumania, which offers a wide range of forward-control light commercials with one- and two-axle drive (4 × 2 and 4 × 4), in addition to some normal-control 4 × 4 models. The 41M microbus (1970 model shown) is of the 4 × 2 type, but can be supplied with four-wheel drive, designated 51M. All models have a 70-bhp four-cylinder petrol engine with four-speed gearbox (plus single-speed transfer box in the case of the 4 × 4 models) and a wheelbase of 2·45 metres. The general design is the same as that used by many manufacturers all over the world. The large wheels help to provide ample ground clearance.

57C TV41M

TWIN COACH, VAN HOOL

58A: Twin Coach TC25S

58B Van Hool/Fiat 625

58A: The **Twin Coach** Division of Highway Products Inc. of Kent, Ohio, USA, offers a variety of rear-engined buses, motor caravans, mobile showrooms, etc., based on two chassis, the 133-in WB TC25 and the 169-in WB TC29. Automatic or manual gearbox, petrol, propane or diesel engine and other options are offered. The vehicle shown is a Suburban or Airporter Coach type with a GVW of 22,000 lb, V8 engine (gasoline or propane), three-speed auto. trans. and air brakes. The 21–29-seat body is of integral construction.

58B: **Van Hool** is one of the leading European bus and coach manufacturers. Based in Koningshooikt, Belgium, various models are produced on proprietary chassis (Bedford, DAF, Ford, Leyland, Mercedes-Benz, Volvo, etc.). For chassisless integral types of their own design the firm uses Fiat engines, axle assemblies, etc. Van Hool was one of the first to offer a purpose-built mini-coach for about 20 passengers, as shown here. It has a 77-SAE-bhp engine, and measures 6·32 by 2·32 metres. 1970.

58C: **Van Hool** medium-sized coach for interior layouts of 29 to 38 seats, based on Fiat mechanical components including 120-SAE-bhp underfloor diesel engine. 1970.

58C Van Hool/Fiat 314

59A: **Vetra** CB45 was one of several trolleybuses produced by the Société des Véhicules & Tracteurs Électriques in Paris immediately after World War II. Of this model there were three variants, Types B, C and D. The 4·60-metre WB 8·75-metre long Type D, which could accommodate 19 seated persons and 26 standees, is shown. The propulsion motor was a 600-Volt 75-hp unit, providing a speed of 50 km/h on the level.
59B: **Vetra** CS60R trolleybus, designed in 1943 and produced in 1945, was similar in external appearance to the CB45. The Type C version had a capacity of 26 seated and up to 36 standing passengers. Wheelbase was 5·00, overall length 9·06 metres. The driving controls and the swivelling driver's seat are shown.
59C: **Vetra** CS60R trolleybus; view of the electrical equipment behind the full-width doors at the front. This model featured rheostatic braking on independent resistance. At 550 Volts, a road speed of 50 km/h could be maintained. The GVW was about 11,300 kg.

59B Vetra CS60R, Type C

59A Vetra CB45, Type D

59C Vetra CS60R, Type C

VETRA

60A: **Vetra** CB60 was a 5·20-m WB trolleybus based on Berliet components and introduced just after the war. With 60 passengers, driver and conductor, the total weight was about 11,500 kg. Road speed at 550 Volts was 60 km/h. The 9.95-metre body was built as an all-metal integral chassis-less unit.
60B: **Vetra** CB60, Type B, interior view, looking forward from the 25-standee rear platform. There was seating for 30 passengers. On the right is the conductor's cabin.
60C: **Vetra** VA3 six-wheeled tandem-drive 12-metre trolleybus, designed to carry 100–140 passengers on city routes. The traction motor produced 130 bhp and voltage varied from 450 to 650. Maximum speed was 55 km/h. The wheelbase was 5·12 + 1·35 metres, the width 2·50 metres. An auxiliary electric motor drove a compressor, providing air pressure for brakes, doors and horn. Many French cities operated Vetras, the largest fleets being in Lyon and Marseille. Vetras were also used in North Africa and some Spanish cities.
60D: **Vetra** VA3 trolleybus at Paris Motor Show, 1947. Visible alongside is a De Dion Bouton coach with rear-mounted six-cylinder opposed-piston diesel engine. (This was one of the last vehicles ever made by this old-established French firm.)

60A Vetra CB60, Type B

60B Vetra CB60, Type B

60C Vetra VA3, Type A

60D Vetra VA3, Type A

61A: The **Volkswagen** Type 2 or 'Transporter' Series embraces all the Company's forward-control commercial models. They have supplemented the Type 1 ('Beetle') car since 1949 and vehicles of similar type were soon introduced by other manufacturers all over the world. The 'Micro Bus' was a luxurious version of the 'Kombi' and is popular in many countries for fast and economical conveyance of groups of up to nine persons. Over the years the Type 2 has had several 'facelifts' and detail improvements. The model shown is of the mid-Sixties. It was also known as the 'Samba'.

61B: **Volvo** B513 bus chassis with Swedish 40-seater bodywork of the mid-Forties. The B513 had 5·20-metre WB and was 9·5 metres long. An 8·75-metre 4·70-metre WB version (B512) was available for 36-seat bodies. Both had a Volvo FE 105-bhp OHV six-cylinder petrol engine, driving through a five-speed overdrive gearbox.

61C: **Volvo** B655 Series underfloor-engined passenger chassis of the early Fifties. The 150-bhp direct-injection horizontal diesel engine was situated behind the front axle and drove through either a five-speed overdrive gearbox or a pre-selective self-change epicyclic gearbox with four forward speeds. There were two wheelbase lengths: 5·50 metres (Model B657) and 6·00 metres (Model B658). They were suitable for bodies of 32 to 54 seats. The bus shown was used in the Swedish city of Uppsala.

61A Volkswagen Type 2 'Micro Bus'

61B Volvo B513

61C Volvo B655 Series

62A Volvo/Hägglund

62B Volvo B59

62C Vulcan 6VF

62A: **Volvo** B58 articulated air passenger bus, produced in conjunction with AB Hägglund & Söner of Örnsköldsvik in the early 1970s. The 185/250-bhp (SAE) underfloor diesel engine is located between the axles of the front unit.
62B: The **Volvo** B59 city bus was introduced in 1971 and is of modern design, featuring a rear-mounted 9·6-litre 230-bhp (DIN) turbo-charged diesel engine with push-button operated automatic transmission (semi-automatic Wilson gearbox available), sub-frame-mounted axles with air suspension, dual-circuit air brakes, power-assisted steering, and other refinements. Operating at half-load, the B59 can reach 25 mph (40 km/h) from standstill in 11 seconds.
62C: **Vulcan** 6VF 13-ft wb export chassis with LHD and bus bodywork of circa 1950. The chassis was first introduced in 1940. It had a 4·57-litre four-cylinder side-valve petrol engine, but in later years a Perkins six-cylinder diesel was available (Model 6PF).

ABBREVIATIONS

auto. trans.	automatic transmission (gearbox)
bhp	brake horsepower
CID	cubic inches displacement
DIN	Deutsche Industrie Norm (Germany)
FC	forward control
GVW	gross vehicle weight
LHD	left-hand drive
LWB	long wheelbase
MoT	Ministry of Transport (GB)
OHV	overhead valves
o-m-o	one-man-operated
PAS	power-assisted steering
RHD	right-hand drive
SAE	Society of Automotive Engineers (USA)
semi-auto.	semi-automatic
SWB	short wheelbase
WB	wheelbase

ACKNOWLEDGEMENTS

This book was compiled and written largely from historic source material in the library of the Olyslager Organisation, and in addition photographs and/or other material was kindly provided or loaned by several individuals and organisations, notably: Mr George Avramidis, Bonallack & Sons Ltd, Mr John Carpenter, Eastern Coach Works Ltd, General Motors Corporation, Mr David Hurley, Karl Kässbohrer Fahrzeugwerke GmbH, Mr Malcolm J. R. Smith and Maschinenfabrik Augsburg-Nürnberg AG.

INDEX

SAN LEANDRO COMMUNITY LIBRARY
SAN LEANDRO, CA 94577